Famous Caves of the World™

Kazumura Cave
The World's Longest Lava Tube

Brad Burnham

The Rosen Publishing Group's
PowerKids Press™
New York

For Pete and Giri

Published in 2003 by The Rosen Publishing Group, Inc.
29 East 21st Street, New York, NY 10010

First Edition

Editor: Nancy MacDonell Smith
Book design: Michael J. Caroleo and Michael De Guzman
Layout design: Eric DePalo

Photo Credits: Cover, title page, pp. 4, 7, 11–12, 15–16, 19 © Dave Bunnell; p. 4 (inset) Nick Sciacca; p. 8 © Douglas Peebles/CORBIS; p. 19 (inset) © Robert Holmes/CORBIS; p. 20 © Reuters NewMedia Inc./CORBIS.

Burnham, Brad.
Kazumura Cave : the world's longest lava tube / Brad Burnham.— 1st ed.
   p. cm. — (Famous caves of the world)
Summary: Provides a tour of Kazumura Cave and some of its natural wonders.
   ISBN 0-8239-6261-X (lib. bdg.)
   1. Kazumura Cave (Hawaii)—Juvenile literature. [1. Kazumura Cave (Hawaii) 2. Caves.]
   I. Title. II. Series.
     GB606.K39 B87 2003
     551.44'7'099691—dc21

                                                        2002000119

Manufactured in the United States of America

Contents

Kauai

Niihau

Oahu

Honolulu

Molokai

Lanai

Kahoolawe

Maui

Pacific Ocean

Hawaiian Islands

Hawaii

Kazumura Cave

World's Longest Lava Cave

Kazumura cave is on the island of Hawaii. It is a long, thin cave that winds its way down the side of a **volcano**, under the surface of the soil. Kazumura cave is long and thin because it was created as **lava** flowed through it. This type of cave is called a lava-tube cave, or lava cave. At about 10 feet (3 m) wide and more than 37 miles (59.5 km) long, Kazumura cave is the longest lava cave in the world.

The lava that made Kazumura cave came from the volcano Kilauea. There are four other volcanoes on the island of Hawaii. Many of them have lava-tube caves, too. Many of the lava-tube caves have been explored, and some are open for people to visit.

Depending on how thick the molten lava was, the surfaces of a lava-tube cave take on different forms. This wall is quite smooth, which means the lava was thick.

Kazumura's Volcano

Kilauea volcano is one of two active volcanoes on the island of Hawaii. The other is Mauna Loa. An active volcano is one that has been **erupting** or that might erupt soon. These volcanoes have been erupting on the island of Hawaii for almost one million years. The eruption that formed Kazumura cave happened hundreds of years ago.

Scientists from the Hawaiian Volcano Observatory study Kilauea. The observatory is on the top of Kilauea next to the Halemaumau **crater**. There are also areas on the sides of Kilauea that have smaller openings. Kazumura cave is in one of these areas, called the East **Rift Zone**.

To get into a lava-tube cave, scientists sometimes need to lower themselves down with long ropes.

Kilauea Erupts

Kazumura cave was made when lava flowed from Kilauea volcano during an eruption. The eruption happened because magma and gases were trapped under Kilauea. Magma is what lava is called when it is still under ground. The magma and gases traveled up to Kilauea from deep in the earth, as deep as 30 miles (48 km). They collected in a large space called a **reservoir**, which is about 3 miles (5 km) under the volcano. The magma and gases filled up the reservoir and then pushed their way out in an eruption.

Most volcanoes on Hawaii have slow, quiet eruptions. These are called Hawaiian-type eruptions. The lava flows slowly down the volcano at about 1,000 feet (305 m) per hour.

Kazumura cave was probably formed during one of Kilauea's Hawaiian-type eruptions. Kilauea is the world's most active volcano.

The Making of a Lava-Tube Cave

Kazumura cave was formed in a lava field. A lava field is the area of ground that lava covers as it flows from a volcano.

As are all lava-tube caves, Kazumura is made of hardened lava. When lava erupts out of a volcano, it moves in a large sheet, the way gravy moves down the sides of mashed potatoes. Sometimes the top layer of lava hardens into solid rock, but **molten** lava continues to flow underneath the rock. The molten lava moves underneath the hardened layer in rivers called lava tubes. After the volcano stops erupting, the lava that is already in the lava tube flows out. The outer layer of hardened lava remains. The empty lava tube is now a lava-tube cave.

Lava blades are formations that stick out from the wall of a lava cave. They look like fins. Lava blades occur in places where the lava flowed more quickly.

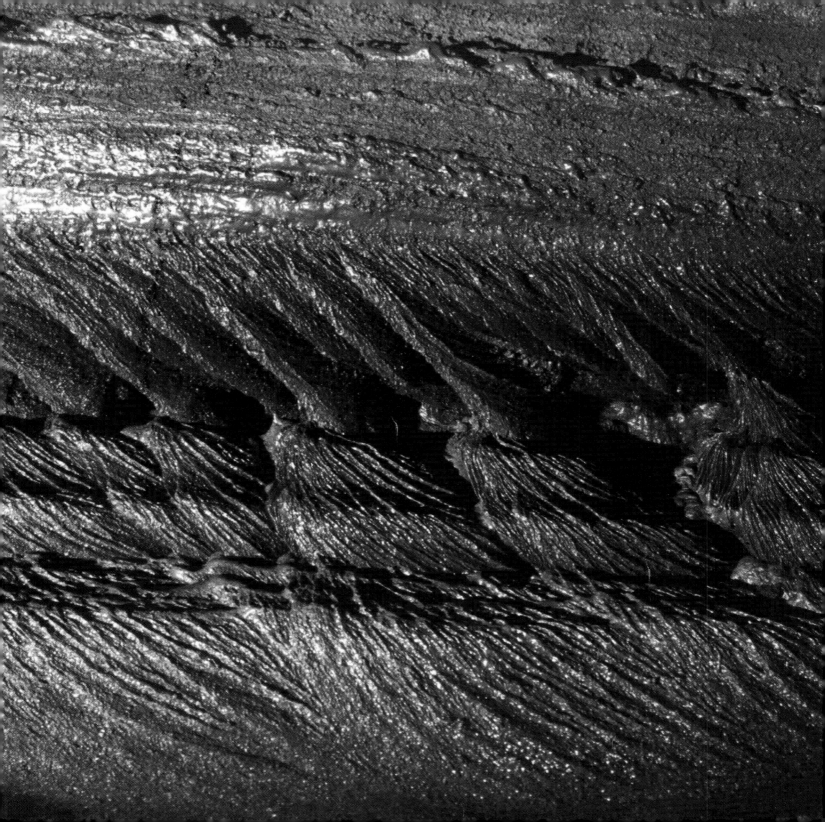

Rough Interior

The walls and floor of Kazumura cave have features in them that give scientists clues about how the lava flowed through the cave. One clue is a **ridge** of hardened lava that is a few feet from the ceiling. It formed as lava on top of the flow attached to the walls and cooled. This tells scientists how high the lava reached when it moved through the cave. The floor of Kazumura cave is made of lava that hardened when the lava stopped flowing. One kind of lava on the floor of Kazumura cave is rope lava. Rope lava has small twists and turns in it that make it look like lengths of rope.

Hardened lava has shapes in it that tell scientists what kind of magma the lava was originally.

Lava Formations

The ceiling of Kazumura cave was shaped by the hot lava and gases that flowed through it. The lava and gases melted parts of the ceiling. When the hot lava left the cave, the melted ceiling cooled and hardened into shapes that look like dripping ice-cream cones. **Stalactites** are the shapes that hang from the ceiling. The stalactites are shaped like icicles, bunches of grapes, large round drops, and strings of beads.

In some places, the ceiling kept dripping after the lava flowed out and created mounds of lava on the floor of the cave. These mounds of hardened lava are called **stalagmites**. Stalagmites can be shaped like tiny volcanoes, candles, and, less often, like roses.

Most of the stalactites in Kazumura cave are just a few inches (cm) long, but they can reach lengths of 3 feet (1 m).

Cave Life

Kazumura cave is a difficult **environment** in which to live. There is no light in the cave, and there are very few sources of food. Some areas of the cave are cool and damp. Other areas of the cave, deep in the earth, are hot and dry. Some areas of the cave even contain deadly gases.

Animals that live in Kazumura cave have **adapted** to this environment. The blind wolf spider and an insect called the blind earwig cannot see, but they are very good at feeling their way around in the cave. Animals like these cannot live outside of the cave and are called **troglodytes**. Other troglodytes include the Big Island cave cricket and the white millipede.

Lava caves are close to Earth's surface. Trees growing above the lava caves send down roots into the cave. Cave insects make their homes in the roots.

A Special Place

Kazumura cave and other areas on Hawaii's volcanoes are **sacred** places for Hawaiians. According to **legends**, the Hawaiian goddess of volcanoes, Pele, lives in Halemaumau crater on top of Kilauea. In these legends, Pele appears as either an old woman or as a beautiful young woman with golden hair. Some people say that they have seen Pele just before a volcanic eruption.

Hawaiians have many **traditions** for honoring special places like Kazumura cave. Hawaiians have used some lava-tube caves as **burial sites**. Lava-tube caves have also been used for everyday activities, such as storing things or creating art. Scientists have found **artifacts** that show these activities.

Lava can be as hot as 2,204°F (1,200°C) when it flows through the lava-tube.
Inset: According to legend, Pele is the daughter of Mother Earth and Father Sky.

Volcanic Islands

The volcanic activity that made Kazumura cave is the same kind that made the Hawaiian islands. The formation of the islands started millions of years ago, when a crack opened up on the ocean floor. The area where this crack is located is called a **hot spot**. Magma came through at the hot spot and started forming mounds of rock on the bottom of the ocean. These mounds were underwater volcanoes. These underwater volcanoes slowly grew upward as more magma erupted from them. Eventually they grew large enough to reach the ocean's surface. When the underwater volcanoes poked through the ocean's surface, they became islands.

When an underwater volcano erupts, the heat from the magma causes a huge cloud of steam to rise up from the ocean.

Hawaii Volcanoes National Park

The Hawaii Volcanoes National Park was created in 1916. The park includes the tops and some of the sides of the two active volcanoes on Hawaii, Mauna Loa and Kilauea. Mauna Loa is 13,160 feet (4,011 m) high, and Kilauea is 3,930 feet (1,198 m) high. Both have erupted in the last 20 years.

The attractions in the park include the Thomas A. Jaggar Museum, views of Kilauea's large crater, and the Thurston lava tube. Recently visitors could also see active lava flows and could feel volcanic activity during their visit. These are the same kinds of volcanic activities that made the Kazumura lava-tube cave hundreds of years ago.

Glossary

adapted (uh-DAP-ted) Changed to fit new conditions.

artifacts (AR-tih-fakts) Objects created and produced by humans.

burial sites (BER-ee-uhl SYTS) Places where bodies are buried.

crater (KRAY-ter) A hole in the ground, shaped like a bowl.

environment (en-VY-urn-ment) The living conditions that make up a place.

erupting (ih-RUPT-ing) Bursting out of something.

hot spot (HAHT SPAHT) A place where molten rock reaches Earth's surface.

lava (LAH-vuh) A hot liquid made of melted rock that comes out of a volcano.

legends (LEH-jendz) Stories that are passed down that many people believe.

molten (MOHL-ten) Something that is made liquid by heat.

reservoir (REH-zuh-vwar) A stored body of liquid.

ridge (RIJ) The long, narrow upper part of something.

rift zone (RIFT ZOHN) When plates break apart and make a crack in Earth's crust.

sacred (SAY-kred) Highly respected and considered very important.

stalactites (stuh-LAK-tyts) Mineral formations that hang down from the ceilings of caves. They can be shaped like icicles.

stalagmites (stuh-LAG-mytz) Mineral formations that rise up from the ground.

traditions (truh-DIH-shuns) Ways of doing things that are passed down through the years.

troglodytes (TRAH-gluh-dyts) Animals that have to live their whole lives in a cave.

volcano (vol-KAY-no) An opening in Earth's surface that sometimes shoots up a hot liquid rock, called lava.

Index

B
Big Island cave cricket, 17
blind wolf spider, 17

H
Halemaumau crater, 6, 18
Hawaiian-type eruptions, 9
Hawaiian Volcanoes National Park, 22
Hawaiian Volcano Observatory, 6
hot spot, 21

K
Kilauea, 5–6, 9, 22

L
lava-tube cave(s), 5, 10, 18, 22

M
magma, 9, 21
Mauna Loa, 6, 22

P
Pele, 18

R
ridge, 13
rope lava, 13

S
scientists, 13
stalactites, 14
stalagmites, 14

T
Thomas A. Jaggar Museum, 22
Thurston lava tube, 22
troglodytes, 17

V
volcano(es), 5–6, 9–10, 14, 18, 21

Web Sites

Due to the changing nature of Internet links, PowerKids Press has developed an online list of Web sites related to the subject of this book. This site is updated regularly. Please use this link to access the list:

www.powerkidspresslink.com/fcow/kazam/